Break Free From Prison: No More Bondage for the Saints

Bill Vincent

Published by RWG Publishing, 2022.

While every precaution has been taken in the preparation of this book, the publisher assumes no responsibility for errors or omissions, or for damages resulting from the use of the information contained herein.

BREAK FREE FROM PRISON: NO MORE BONDAGE FOR THE SAINTS

First edition. August 31, 2022.

Copyright © 2022 Bill Vincent.

Written by Bill Vincent.

Also by Bill Vincent

Building a Prototype Church: Divine Strategies Released
Experience God's Love: By Revival Waves of Glory School of the Supernatural
Glory: Expanding God's Presence
Glory: Increasing God's Presence
Glory: Kingdom Presence of God
Glory: Pursuing God's Presence
Glory: Revival Presence of God
Rapture Revelations: Jesus Is Coming
The Prototype Church: Heaven's Strategies for Today's Church
The Secret Place of God's Power
Transitioning Into a Prototype Church: New Church Arising
Spiritual Warfare Made Simple
Aligning With God's Promises
A Closer Relationship With God
Armed for Battle: Spiritual Warfare Battle Commands
Breakthrough of Spiritual Strongholds
Desperate for God's Presence: Understanding Supernatural Atmospheres
Destroying the Jezebel Spirit: How to Overcome the Spirit Before It Destroys You!
Discerning Your Call of God

Glory: Expanding God's Presence: Discover How to Manifest God's Glory

Glory: Kingdom Presence Of God: Secrets to Becoming Ambassadors of Christ

Satan's Open Doors: Access Denied

Spiritual Warfare: The Complete Collection

The War for Spiritual Battles: Identify Satan's Strategies

Understanding Heaven's Court System: Explosive Life Changing Secrets

A Godly Shaking: Don't Create Waves

Faith: A Connection of God's Power

Global Warning: Prophetic Details Revealed

Overcoming Obstacles

Spiritual Leadership: Kingdom Foundation Principles

Glory: Revival Presence of God: Discover How to Release Revival Glory

Increasing Your Prophetic Gift: Developing a Pure Prophetic Flow

Millions of Churches: Why Is the World Going to Hell?

The Supernatural Realm: Discover Heaven's Secrets

The Unsearchable Riches of Christ: Chosen to be Sons of God

Deep Hunger: God Will Change Your Appetite Toward Him

Defeating the Demonic Realm

Glory: Increasing God's Presence: Discover New Waves of God's Glory

Growing In the Prophetic: Developing a Prophetic Voice

Healing After Divorce: Grace, Mercy and Remarriage

Love is Waiting

Awakening of Miracles: Personal Testimonies of God's Healing Power

Deception and Consequences Revealed: You Shall Know the Truth and the Truth Shall Set You Free

Overcoming the Power of Lust

Are You a Follower of Christ: Discover True Salvation

Cover Up and Save Yourself: Revealing Sexy is Not Sexy

Heaven's Court System: Bringing Justice for All

The Angry Fighter's Story: Harness the Fire Within

The Wrestler: The Pursuit of a Dream

Beginning the Courts of Heaven: Understanding the Basics

Breaking Curses: Legal Rights in the Courts of Heaven

Writing and Publishing a Book: Secrets of a Christian Author

How to Write a Book: Step by Step Guide

The Anointing: Fresh Oil of God's Presence

Spiritual Leadership: Kingdom Foundation Principles Second Edition

The Courts of Heaven: How to Present Your Case

The Jezebel Spirit: Tactics of Jezebel's Control

Heaven's Angels: The Nature and Ranking of Angels

Don't Know What to Do?: Discover Promotion in the Wilderness

Word of the Lord: Prophetic Word for 2020

The Coronavirus Prophecy

Increase Your Anointing: Discover the Supernatural

Apostolic Breakthrough: Birthing God's Purposes

The Healing Power of God: Releasing the Power of the Holy Spirit

The Secret Place of God's Power: Revelations of God's Word

The Rapture: Details of the Second Coming of Christ

Increase of Revelation and Restoration: Reveal, Recover & Restore

Restoration of the Soul: The Presence of God Changes Everything

Building a Prototype Church: The Church is in a Season of Profound of Change

Keys to Receiving Your Miracle: Miracles Happen Today

The Resurrection Power of God: Great Exploits of God

Transitioning to the Prototype Church: The Church is in a Season of Profound of Transition

Waves of Revival: Expect the Unexpected

The Stronghold of Jezebel: A True Story of a Man's Journey

Glory: Pursuing God's Presence: Revealing Secrets

Like a Mighty Rushing Wind

Steps to Revival

Supernatural Power

The Goodness of God

The Secret to Spiritual Strength

The Glorious Church's Birth: Understanding God's Plan For Our Lives

God's Presence Has a Profound Impact On Us

Spiritual Battles of the Mind: When All Hell Breaks Loose, Heaven Sends Help

A Godly Shaking Coming to the Church: Churches are Being Rerouted

Relationship with God in a New Way

The Spirit of God's Anointing: Using the Holy Spirit's Power in You

The Magnificent Church: God's Power Is Being Manifested

Miracles Are Awakened: Today is a Day of Miracles

Prepared to Fight: The Battle of Deliverance

The Journey of a Faithful: Adhering to the teachings of Jesus Christ

Ascension to the Top of Spiritual Mountains: Putting an End to Pain Cycles

After Divorce Recovery: When I Think of Grace, I Think of Mercy and Remarriage

A Greater Sense of God's Presence: Learn How to Make God's Glory Visible

Do Not Allow the Enemy to Steal: To a Crown of Righteousness, a Crown of Thorns

There Are Countless Churches: What is the Cause of Global Doom?

Creating a Model Church: The Church is Undergoing Considerable Upheaval

Developing Your Prophetic Ability: Creating a Flow of Pure Prophetic Intent

Christ's Limitless Riches Are Unsearchable: God Has Chosen Us to Be His Sons

Faith is a Link Between God's Might and Ours

Increasing the Presence of God: The Revival of the End-Times Is Approaching

Getting a Prophecy for Yourself: Unlocking Your Prophecies with Prophetic Keys

Getting Rid of the Jezebel Spirit: Before the Spirit Destroys You, Here's How to Overcome It!

Getting to Know Heaven's Court System: Secrets That Will Change Your Life

God's Resurrected Presence: Revival Glory is Being Released

God's Presence In His Kingdom: Secrets to Becoming Christ's Ambassadors

God's Healing Ability: The Holy Spirit's Power is Being Released

God's Power of Resurrection: God's Great Exploits

Heaven's Supreme Court: Providing Equal Justice for All

Increasing God's Presence in Our Lives: God's Glory Has Reached New Heights

Jezebel's Stronghold: This is the Story of an Actual Man's Journey

Making the Shift to the Model Church: The Church Is In the Midst of a Major Shift

Overcoming Lust's Influence: The Way to Victory

Pursuing God's Presence: Disclosing Information

The Plan to Take Over America: Restoring, We the People and the Power of God

Revelation and Restoration Are Increasing: The Process That Reveals, Recovers, and Restores

Burn In the Presence of the Lord

Revival Tidal Waves: Be Prepared for the Unexpected

Taking down the Demonic Realm: Curses and Revelations of Demonic Spirits

The Apocalypse: Details about Christ's Second Coming

The Hidden Resource of God's Power

The Open Doors of Satan: Access is Restricted

The Secrets to Getting Your Miracle

The Truth About Deception and Its Consequences

The Universal World: Discover the Mysteries of Heaven

Warning to the World: Details of Prophecies Have Been Revealed

Wonders and Significance: God's Glory in New Waves

Word of the Lord

Why Is There No Lasting Revival: It's Time For the Next Move of God

A Double New Beginning: A Prophetic Word, the Best Is Yet to Come

Your Most Productive Season Ever: The Anointing to Get Things Done

Break Free From Prison: No More Bondage for the Saints

Breaking Strongholds: Taking Steps to Freedom

Carrying the Glory of God: Igniting the End Time Revival

Breakthrough Over the Enemies Attack on Resources: An Angel Called Breakthrough

Days of Breakthrough: Your Time is Now

Empowered For the Unprecedented: Extraordinary Days Ahead

The Ultimate Guide to Self-Publishing: How to Write, Publish, and Promote Your Book for Free

The Art of Writing: A Comprehensive Guide to Crafting Your Masterpiece

The Non-Fiction Writer's Guide: Mastering Engaging Narratives

Spiritual Leadership (Large Print Edition): Kingdom Foundation Principles

Desperate for God's Presence (Large Print Edition): Understanding Supernatural Atmospheres

From Writer to Marketer: How to Successfully Promote Your Self-Published Book

Unleashing Your Inner Author: A Step-by-Step Guide to Crafting Your Own Bestseller

Becoming a YouTube Sensation: A Guide to Success

Watch for more at https://revivalwavesofgloryministries.com/.

Break Free From Prison: No More Bondage for the Saints

SUMMARY KEYWORDS
prison, God, healed, faith, life, healing, free, understand, Jesus, failure, prison doors, freedom

The opening of the prison. Have you ever felt like you've been in prison? You've been spending some time there recently? I don't know about you, but it's time to get out. God has given us a Get Out of Jail Free Code.

Isaiah 61 and Luke 4:18 talks about things to do with the opening of the prison, the opening of the prison some of us have a coffin prison. And it is God's figurative illustration of the release of imprisonment It's an imprisonment something you've been held captive. It could be sickness; it could be sin can be everything and anything. Anything that happened and could have come upon our lives in the fall, is a prison when Adam and Eve fell everything that they open that door to becomes a prison in our life and it covers every phase of our redemption and our salvation. And what I have to say applies equally to every bondage known, there is no bondage that is not known that we're coming in that we're not supposed to be free of, and I'm telling you if you are physically well and your problem is one of the many others then think of your problem as an open prison and we're going to follow instructions and I believe that God's given us. He's given us instructions to get out of prison we're not going to have to make a pic out of a toothbrush we're not going to have to use the spoon that we had in the cafeteria and use that to dig our way out like some of those bad prison movies, but you can keep God busy filling his promises for you.

See have you ever been assaulted, bound by something in your life? And then you finally get free. And sometimes you don't realize you're free right away, do you? You've lived at home so long you've lived in that prison so long that sometimes it's like you walk out of prison you're walking around you're thinking all right, Where're the guards? It's been known that many men especially men that I have heard of when they've been in prison for more than 10 years, get out of prison. They don't know what to do. They feel like anything at any moment is going to take them back into prison. And some of them do something to get back into prison because they forget how to live. The same thing happens with us. When you've been bound up for so long Oh, you knew I was going to flip this. You've been bound up for so long with something in your life when you finally get free from it almost don't know how to live unless you have it. So, some people put themselves back in prison doors.

When I saw by the Spirit of God today it was like the old Andy Griffith Show. But they had one of the most insecure jails in the world. They hung the key outside the cell. And many times, Otis would come staggering in, if you know the show. He was a town drunk. And he comes staggering in check himself into jail. Staggering and grabbing the key, unlock it, and let himself in the next morning when he's sober. He'd unlock it and let himself go. And I want you to understand that sometimes I feel like we're all still in Mayberry right now. And we are in prison, but we're in the prison that we are allowing ourselves to be in. We can get out anytime the keys are right there. But we don't want to use the key because we don't want to get out of there and be free from this thing. Some people have not known what freedom is. But when you find out that you've gotten free, you change your tone you started thinking, like when I got healed on my ankle.

I know I experienced days of not even knowing when I got healed. How do you even know that you're not healed? When you have pain, agonizing pain every day? How do you not know that you're not healed? See you live in abundance. See, I was in a prison. I'm still using a cane. I was still limping. It was so long that I just did what I always did.

See, sometimes we get to the place where we think we don't know what freedom is. Like I said earlier, we've all come from all kinds of different things, but we have come so far, and much of our life we've come out of is prison. So, what does it mean by opening the prison? It means prisoners are free, the guards of the prison will walk you to the gate unlock the gate and let you out.

And in some states, they give you a new suit and a little bit of cash. First, I don't know how far you're going to go as an ex-con. But anyway, that's their rehabilitation but just imagine for a moment when they're free they're finally free. They look back and they see the barbed wire they see the change they see the fence they see the guard towers sometimes as well we are free that's the way we are free. We are walking out of the prison and we're like I know I'm healed. I know I'm here but we're looking back at the gate they think how far before they pick us off. To tell prisoners that they are free. Tell the captors that they are released. See Jesus open the prison for us by burying the punishment.

It's like we did something so bad that we should be locked up and then once they find out that we know Jesus that we found Jesus they find out this and they come to the prison door open it up and say sorry you're not supposed to be here. We need to let you out. Why did you do the crime? Yes, I did. But you found Jesus and you repented of that. So, because of that, I got I need to release you. So, once you understand, Jehovah has called to meet on Him the punishment for all of us. That's what the Bible says, In Deuteronomy 28. All sickness is listed among the punishments. Did you hear me, all sickness is listed in the punishments of it.

Jesus paid our debt. As it says it does not have to be paid twice or for free.

We're free most of us need to understand, that one of the number one things, it's going to cause us to go into total prison is faith. Say I don't believe we're never supposed to forget where we've come from.

We never forget where we've come from. People don't even know what hard life is anymore. They do not have a clue what real hard life is. And I want you to understand that God is about to open the prison doors He's about to cause you to be free. Do you want to be free?

See, when you find true freedom you rest. How many know somebody who's been in prison for many years, you don't sleep.

You don't really rest. You might close your eyes, and you might do a little snoring from time to time, but your sleep is not resting. And when you finally get out of prison, you're free. You're totally cut off from any bondage whatsoever. You're going to enter a place of rest where you're not going to be concerned or worried about any of your past. I came out of a hard life. I've come out of a hard family, I came out of a lot of stuff, to where you're taught to lie. You're taught to deceive, you're taught to manipulate, you're taught to be a womanizer, you're taught to do all this stuff. And so, when I came out of that stuff, and I started

BREAK FREE FROM PRISON: NO MORE BONDAGE FOR THE SAINTS

getting saved, I got saved. There's a difference. Some people get saved, and some people get delivered and saved. In other words, I got saved and I just thought Jesus was in my life, but I had a lot of stuff still battling every day, and I still battled it every day. And I'm telling you when I finally found a lot of freedom to almost anything I could ever think of because God's always dealing with you. I found freedom as I had never known before. To where I didn't have to worry. Have ever had secrets in your life to where you're like, oh, man, I forgot what I lied about? I forgot what I did. Liars usually lie so much. They forget what the lie was. They have one lie with their mom, they have another lie. They have another lie. It's like, all right, which one do we want to do? Which one did I tell you? I'm telling you, and when you find our freedom, suddenly, it's like, wait a minute, I don't have anything to hide. I don't have anything to worry about. I don't have to look over my shoulder anymore. I don't have to worry that somebody's going to find anything. That's a freedom that nobody realizes you need until you finally get it.

See, Jesus used the word bound, when he said, ought not this woman who Satan hath bound, be loosed. When we are bound up. We're in prison. Some people get kicked, captured, or held hostage in something and they get bound up and put into a room. To them that's prison. They don't have to call it some certain prison. They don't have to title it anything. It's a prison because they're bound up. You can be chained to a tree and that becomes a prison. You can be chained to something else and that can become a prison you can be locked in the trunk of a car that can become a prison. The same thing goes for spiritual things we become a prisoner. Some people are riddled with fear.

So the thing that's going to help us the most and get out of prison and stay out of prison is right thinking and right believing that's the two things - right thinking and right believing because after knowing that the prison is open because that's the first thing we need to understand, the prison doors are open we've been given access to the doors open when Jesus paid the price all the prison doors were opened. Some people are just choosing to stay there. Sometimes you will be going along in your life and have no problem whatsoever and then somebody flips a switch. Anybody can have a switch? It's like a light switch turns your darkness on. Do you know what I just meant by that?

Our thoughts are supposed to be to the obedience of Christ. We're supposed to clean up our thinking. Since the natural man Adam and Eve fell, we by law have been imprisoned. Come home. And what that does is it causes us to look for symptoms. Today's commercials are nasty. They're nasty.

They'll talk about medication and tell you how sick you can be. You may have this, this, this, and this. It's like well, wonderful. See, the opening of the prison frees us from bondage making it impossible to see and know beyond our natural senses. In other words, we're not going to let things register that will cause us to be sick. See, no matter how sick a person ever gets, there's a part of us that must accept it. Because if we don't, I'm talking about there's a lot of people that are sick, as sick as they are because they've accepted to stay sick. Some people even doctors will tell you a spring ankle can be healed within a matter of days, even a couple of weeks. But some people can turn it into a lifetime of injury here's the thing I'm going to try to get through, I hope you can receive this the way that I heard it today. Faith needs no evidence, but the Word of God faith requires no evidence except

BREAK FREE FROM PRISON: NO MORE BONDAGE FOR THE SAINTS

the word. See, it is blind to all things. As I said, most of the battle this ministry and everyone in it is doing right now is waiting and it's like waiting when it's two degrees outside and you're waiting for the bus outside. It doesn't matter if you wait five minutes or 15 minutes or an hour. It doesn't matter how long you wait. It is unwelcome news to be waiting. See, we look not at the things which are seen. That's what faith is. Faith only sees the Word of God. It doesn't see anything else. When we rely upon physical evidence Hello, faith when we only rely on physical evidence, faith has no opportunity to exercise itself. When we only rely on physical evidence, faith has no opportunity to exercise itself. We are in the seen world we constantly rely on what we can see while faith is on what we cannot see. We like to rely on what we have when faith is what we have not yet.

See, let him forsake his thoughts. My thought would be if I have no money, I must have no money. A man's thoughts have been the prison is locked.

Faith is your free See, he must forsake such thoughts and think the truth. And the truth is the prison is open. And therefore, he can walk free.

Some people can think that the thing they are dealing with is going to kill them another person can have the same issue and can think and believe they're going to be healed. Now is one wrong?

It can be a deadly disease.

And I'm not saying the Mind over Matter thing. I'm not trying to say that we just get all new age and say, well, you know, if I find that I got something wrong with me, I'm just going to go Oh, no, I don't. But what I am saying is there's a level of faith that causes things that don't exist to exist. And if we just accept death, we fast forward to death.

Now I want you to understand that.

See, especially when we have a promise, Faith stands on the Word of God. And the sick man must forsake his way of judging according to the walls of the prison. When you're in prison, you judge a certain way weren't you, you live a certain way. But see, when you're free, you're no longer in prison. As soon as the good news, that's why they call it good news. Because we get out of prison.

So, the good news is, believed when good news is believed it produces joy.

He has sent me to preach the acceptable year of the Lord. The gospel age was typified in the Old Testament, a Jubilee. It's a time of shouting. It's a time of freedom. See, it was a happy year because God said on the Day of Atonement that in this 50th year, you shall return every man to his possessions. See, it is a time for rejoicing. God is bringing a season of restoration right now. He's taken us out of prison and put us back into all the possessions and more. So, in other words, everything that's ever been stolen from you, everything that's ever been robbed from you, the years that you have lost are going to be restored unto you

God promises when we genuinely believe become the rejoicing of our hearts before they are fulfilled to us. See, when you believe you should have a joyful heart before it even happens. That's what real faith is.

That's what real faith is.

Real faith is your joy before it even happens. This is something to be excited about and upset about at the same time. Because we are the waiting generation God is doing something.

BREAK FREE FROM PRISON: NO MORE BONDAGE FOR THE SAINTS

He's always moving forward. Things are coming faster than they've ever come. We're right now I know as far as our house, we are getting bigger blessings, bigger releases, and bigger things are coming. I can see a lot of things that are on the way.

Every day that it's not there is a day that it's closer. Every day that is not there is a day that is closer.

Imagine for a moment a guy in prison, he has no chance for parole, no chance to get out. The governor gives him a pardon. Imagine for a moment that this guy was not just in jail, but he was in the electric chair. If you're in the electric chair, and you get a pardon from the governor, talking about missing something. Talk about realization settling in talking about the prison doors opening. Suddenly the electric chair is about to be electrocuted. And the governor calls on the phone and says I want to pardon this guy. Before the guy even gets up from that chair, there's going to be a joy, we are free of being out of prison. He finds out that He's pardoned. He's still in prison. He's still in bondage. He's still being walked by guards. And as he goes through the prison, getting dressed, getting ready, the more he gets ready to get out of that jail, the more he gets joy. And that's what it's like sometimes with us, we are knowing that we're getting free. We know that is coming. We're believing God and we're getting joyful about it. It just hasn't manifested. Because it's that waiting. I believe right now, waiting. And what we are dealing with right now is a lot of waiting. It's like a transition on loop. And if you don't know what a loop is I'm talking about, you know, like, have you played music and you just want to put on a loop? It just keeps playing over and over and repeatedly. Transition is like, Oh, here's a turn transition. I'm transitioning from this place to this place to this place.

The absence of rejoicing would prove that you're not believing that you're getting out of prison. I want you to understand that sometimes faith looks like they're joyful and happy Why are they joyful and happy if they don't have anything they're not doing that good that's why sometimes when we keep a good attitude and positive and promising and believing God and joyful that things are getting closer and closer there's a bigger breakthrough

I hope you catch this I hope you cache that a sick person must forsake the thought that his freedom is a future act did you hear what I said? A sick person must forsake his freedom is a future act because it's not a future act it's a past act you were healed before you got sick it was paid for before you got it. We're believing God for something in the future when sometimes it's already been. God says I'll supply all your needs according to His riches and glory. You're looking this way maybe you're looking the other way maybe our trains are in reverse. Try to get this. See the door of your prison has been open for a long time so you just say Jesus come into my life forgive me for my sins and you keep that up, your prison door was open. If you've got a little sin in your life the key was right, there see by His stripes you were healed what? I'm going to say something.

The Emancipation Proclamation by Abraham Lincoln made the slaves of the South free before they knew they were free some of them were still in prison. Some were still doing the job. I bet you when somebody came up as a hey, hey, hey, hey, you're free. I bet he goes. No, you're free. You can just go; you don't have to do that. I bet some of them didn't know how to stop.

They did not know they were free because the proclamation was released. They were pardoned but they still were acting as if they were in prison so, by the time they got out of prison, it was past tense.

They did not use their freedom until they were informed of it.

They did not judge according to their surrounding but by the proclamation. The opening of the prison has made you free. You will be imprisoned until you walk out.

God's Word says that it is as dead as a body without a spirit is dead. I want you to understand no one else can do your part for you. Have you ever gotten delivered or something and picked it back up? Jesus commanded the blind man with a withered hand to stretch or stretch it forth.

I used to see Brother Denny (Dr. Dennis Goodell) all the time, tell somebody that was twisted up in their body sitting in a wheelchair and he says rise and walk, and they look at him like Are you for real? Sometimes I like to just get bold and say what are you here for? Why does somebody come to a healing service or miracle crusade or thing unless you're believing God is going to touch your life? Even in the Old Testament times of Jonah sacrifice with the voice of thanksgiving calling his prison walls lying vanities not after but before he got out, was needed to dip in Jordan seven times before his leprosy was cleansed. Say they were in prison, but they had to in something themselves to get out of prison.

Would you ask yourself right now to pray yourself out of prison? Sometimes you got to say come on bill get up and get going.

Sometimes you could just lay there and wither up and die. We got to fix our eyes on one thing. That's the open door. And the walls of your prison will soon be behind you. The manifestation of everything you've been believing God for will be upon you.

Are you ready for that?

We cannot accept failure. The enemy wants you to be a failure. The enemy wants you to fail.

God wants to get you out of prison. But I'm talking about after prison. This is what I'm talking about. After you get out of prison. We cannot accept failure. What are the most painful things is a person who has all his faith pinned up on the success or failure of someone else? We can pin everything in our life all up for somebody else.

When we go to heaven, nobody's going to be able to get in because of something I've done. I'm not going to be able to go because of something that somebody else has done. We're going to get there and be able to get in by what we have done in our own right. Sometimes we get so built up, that we pin all our success and our failure on someone else. In other words, if we don't make it, it's our mom and dad's fault.

It's a pitiful thing for us to just base our life because of something somebody else did. You know, a lot of people in my family failed.

They did not even graduate high school and did not have any success in their life whatsoever. I'm a living testimony just by existing into things of God the way I am. I'm a living testimony.

But there are people I know in your family, my family and ourselves included, who try to blame our success or our failure on somebody else. know like, if this one over here, hypothetically, gets in trouble or gets a bad grade on something. They try to compare themselves to this one over here. Well, guess what? This one over here is not her. We cannot base our success or our failure on anybody else.

That is. Failure.

The faith that receives things from God is the faith that cometh by hearing the Word of God. Instead of seeing a failure, we hear the word of God, all of us hear it, but we don't do anything. We got a whole bunch of people who hear it all the time. But it's one thing to hear it. It's another thing to do.

Here's a question that is often asked. I know a saint that's been afflicted for many years. She has faith. She's prayed earnestly for her deliverance. But so many of God's best men of God have prayed for her. And there's no change in her condition. She lives so close to God, and it looks like she will receive her healing. What's the matter with her? Why doesn't she receive her healing? Have you ever had that thought either in your mind or heard somebody say? They do the same thing everybody else does, but they don't seem to get healed. I want to stay here just for a moment because this is where the devil likes to just rule and reign in a believer to make them a non-believer. Just know doubt is a demon. A demon will rule your life and it will cause you to almost want to prove God isn't doing anything. I've had people part of our group. They have gone to meetings with us. They've traveled and gone places and they went to other ministers' meetings, and they've been closed and they literally, were trying to prove that their life was falling apart despite the words. In other words, they tried to expect failure to prove the word wrong. Sounds twisted, doesn't it? Why would you want to prove that something is wrong? It's a demon.

It's a demon that does it. And I'm telling you sometimes we get so caught up in trying to prove somebody wrong that we don't even try to prove it. We don't even try to do something right. And I'm telling you, we can get so caught up and losing and failure, that's what it is, it's a failure. We set ourselves up for failure. One person set, their whole life right now is set up on a spirit of failure.

I knew a man. He did not believe in divine healing, did not believe in it whatsoever. These are stories, God said, I want you to talk about just for a moment because it's going to break something off somebody. But he would try to get a phone number of somebody who got healed in service, to try to convince them it wasn't. It didn't happen. This was a minister. And so, he would call them and try to convince them they were not healed. And he says that the man told him that he had his healing but lost it. So of course, he jumped on that. The minister thought he was right. Even though he was trying to convince people that they weren't healed.

Trying to pull down the belief that you could be healed, set free delivered, but didn't believe in it. So, he was trying to get everybody else not to believe in it either. Now, if I was a different man, then like I am now this man would not have made it 10 feet. But back then I was gentle and gave him a lot of grace.

But he tried to use this one failure, where the man lost his healing, to prove that there was nothing to the 1000s of healings that happened in the same crusade. So, he started advertising that 1000s were being healed in a crusade and he tried to convince one man that lost his healing to discount the rest of them. See, at the same time, we can find a man out of 1000 that received salvation and lost it and find 1000s that gets saved and keep it, does that prove that there's no salvation? I'm going there for a reason. So, what I want you to understand is we cannot accept failure.

When we lose something that's a failure.

I get mad at the devil when he tries to put some back on my life. Have you ever gotten mad at the devil when he tries to put something back on your life? Do You reclaim whatever the devil is trying to steal from you? I believe God will prove His work. He'll prove himself faithful.

The promise of salvation, even if no one ever takes advantage of it, is true. The same truth is true for healing. The promise for healing is there even if nobody ever claims it?

The same is true for the Holy Ghost. Just because one person fails somewhere, does not mean it's a failure for all.

I went to a service where a guy did not believe in healing. Then he gave God an ultimatum. He said if this woman in a wheelchair gets up and walks tonight, I'll go up front and get saved. That woman didn't just get up and walk, she ran up and down the aisle. She'd been in her wheelchair since she was nine years old. She was like 60. This was a miraculous event, this young man was just sitting there like, oh my goodness, he goes up and he goes to pray. And suddenly, everything, in his life just came out, suddenly come to find out. He was a very evil, young man because he would always try to get people convinced God wasn't real. So, I want you to understand something, no matter what doubt and extreme things come.

We cannot always believe the lie. No, not everything they say in the media is true. You can't believe it all. You know, it used to be only that one certain magazine at the end of the grocery aisle was the only one that was false.

The reason I'm saying this is because we've gotten to the point where we are coming to the end of times. And that doubt and unbelief are going to be put out, they're is so much for everybody. It's going to be just like, the politics going on. On one side, Hillary can do 10 - 15 things and immediately gives like 10 minutes of airtime about it. Trump can do one thing. And they'll make a whole weekend feature of this event. Because it's one-sided. It's all about, let's try to tear this one down more. The thing is something is going to happen with the media. All that's going on with the things of God is whenever you see one miracle take place, and 1000s come into a crusade, there's going to be immediate people that are going to try to twist it and try to magnify all the ones that don't get saved. All the ones that don't get healed. We're going to have to be able to stand strong through it all and not accept failure, not accept a lie, not accept anything else. God is still healing. God is still delivering. God still is doing miracle signs and wonders no matter what anyone says. One man told me one time, you can never trust the media. They will put on a smiley face and tell you they want to do this great interview and help you advertise the revival; help you get free publicity and all kinds of stuff even offering you money. But everything will be desperately wicked, there's going to be an underhanded thing. See, if a doctor tells you not to eat green peaches. I'm going somewhere with this, green peaches. Then you should remove the calls of that before you get cured. Because if you don't take doctors' medicine sometimes and advice then many times you won't be cured

I believe sometimes we remove the cause and investigate the Word. See, God can heal some of us of different things. But guess what that means we got to change something.

BREAK FREE FROM PRISON: NO MORE BONDAGE
FOR THE SAINTS

See, move the cause of the affliction and the healing comes.

Sin is not the cause of sickness. Some refused to lay hold on the promise of God. It seems that some good people trust their doctors, or the Lord Some people believe you're supposed to suffer it out. Just suffer it out.

I'm going somewhere with this. Some Christians are stubborn and will not obey the Lord. God will tell one person don't eat ice. They cannot live without that ice. If God tells you to stop something, there's a reason for you. You don't always have to know why. God tells you to take an aspirin a day for a week, two weeks, or three weeks. There's a reason for God to use the medicine. God will tell you to take certain vitamins, go ahead, and do that. God tells you to stop drinking coffee, you do that God says stop eating that you do that. If God doesn't tell you, you just keep going. No.

We don't want to obey anybody. You know, we don't want to obey anybody. For some people, God said, You need to soak your feet. You need to do this, this, and this. You say Oh God could have healed that. Yeah, but see, He gave a prescription instead of Him just doing a quick miracle. He said soak your feet just like He said to the one to dip seven times.

Why because sometimes I believe we always want the effortless way out.

My last point. We don't need to rely on people. You're only relying on God. You cannot rely on anybody in your life. Nobody. You can thank God for your husband, thank God for your wife, and thank God for your children. Thank God for your children and you might have a lot of things going on there, but don't rely on people. Why? Some receive healing when others don't. When the person they are watching fails many times to get healed. They won't get healed either. I've seen people who base their deliverance and their healings and everything. Hang it on somebody else. One won't worship and gets set on fire until the other one does. If one would step up the other one would follow. It didn't matter who, that's the way it would work.

God doesn't go back on His promises, but we go back on ours. Have You ever prayed the prayer, God Get me out of this mess and I will serve you the rest of my days. A lot of people pray that prayer and they leave God high and dry.

See when you fail to be saved because there is a hypocrite here or there, you lose.

There is a mentality right now that we are just defending our life many times on somebody else.

I know husbands who are waiting for their wives to get on fire. Just waiting. Waiting for their wife to finally get her head out of her butt and what it's done it's pulled him down. Waiting will get you dead. Waiting is like waiting on a street corner in North St. Louis.

Well, I'm just waiting for my wife. She says she is coming I'm just waiting. Especially if I was standing in the corner indoors, they lose all the memories in my life that are going to get me out of that mess. I'll tell you hopefully, as well just start praying.

I'm telling you people base their life on this. There are a lot of wives that are going to church right now and they're just waiting on their husbands to rise they're not going to go any farther in the things of God because they're waiting you know what? If I ever did anything to fall when I pray my wife will just take off like a rocket. And it is things that God leave me behind and make me want it

Oh, that's a good pastor's wife. Oh, yeah, I'm not a pastor.

BREAK FREE FROM PRISON: NO MORE BONDAGE FOR THE SAINTS

Are you ready for the increase that God's about to bring, He is about to bring an abundance of increase? It's got to come with a lot of garbage, but it's going to come with a lot of glories. God is going to clean up a lot of mess. We need to be able to rise out of the ashes out of the junk out of the stuff. Right now, God's coming back for our glorious Church, and we're supposed to be part of that glorious Church. He'll set free delivery, not being swayed this way or that. And even when everybody does a spin on something to try to make it not be believable, we're going to still believe we're still going to stand in it. And we're going to still know, for a matter of fact, that God is the God of miracles

Are you ready to get out of our ruts and get out of our prison? Finally. It's time for freedom.

Also by Bill Vincent

Building a Prototype Church: Divine Strategies Released
Experience God's Love: By Revival Waves of Glory School of the Supernatural
Glory: Expanding God's Presence
Glory: Increasing God's Presence
Glory: Kingdom Presence of God
Glory: Pursuing God's Presence
Glory: Revival Presence of God
Rapture Revelations: Jesus Is Coming
The Prototype Church: Heaven's Strategies for Today's Church
The Secret Place of God's Power
Transitioning Into a Prototype Church: New Church Arising
Spiritual Warfare Made Simple
Aligning With God's Promises
A Closer Relationship With God
Armed for Battle: Spiritual Warfare Battle Commands
Breakthrough of Spiritual Strongholds
Desperate for God's Presence: Understanding Supernatural Atmospheres
Destroying the Jezebel Spirit: How to Overcome the Spirit Before It Destroys You!
Discerning Your Call of God

Glory: Expanding God's Presence: Discover How to Manifest God's Glory

Glory: Kingdom Presence Of God: Secrets to Becoming Ambassadors of Christ

Satan's Open Doors: Access Denied

Spiritual Warfare: The Complete Collection

The War for Spiritual Battles: Identify Satan's Strategies

Understanding Heaven's Court System: Explosive Life Changing Secrets

A Godly Shaking: Don't Create Waves

Faith: A Connection of God's Power

Global Warning: Prophetic Details Revealed

Overcoming Obstacles

Spiritual Leadership: Kingdom Foundation Principles

Glory: Revival Presence of God: Discover How to Release Revival Glory

Increasing Your Prophetic Gift: Developing a Pure Prophetic Flow

Millions of Churches: Why Is the World Going to Hell?

The Supernatural Realm: Discover Heaven's Secrets

The Unsearchable Riches of Christ: Chosen to be Sons of God

Deep Hunger: God Will Change Your Appetite Toward Him

Defeating the Demonic Realm

Glory: Increasing God's Presence: Discover New Waves of God's Glory

Growing In the Prophetic: Developing a Prophetic Voice

Healing After Divorce: Grace, Mercy and Remarriage

Love is Waiting

Awakening of Miracles: Personal Testimonies of God's Healing Power

Deception and Consequences Revealed: You Shall Know the Truth and the Truth Shall Set You Free

Overcoming the Power of Lust

Are You a Follower of Christ: Discover True Salvation

Cover Up and Save Yourself: Revealing Sexy is Not Sexy

Heaven's Court System: Bringing Justice for All

The Angry Fighter's Story: Harness the Fire Within

The Wrestler: The Pursuit of a Dream

Beginning the Courts of Heaven: Understanding the Basics

Breaking Curses: Legal Rights in the Courts of Heaven

Writing and Publishing a Book: Secrets of a Christian Author

How to Write a Book: Step by Step Guide

The Anointing: Fresh Oil of God's Presence

Spiritual Leadership: Kingdom Foundation Principles Second Edition

The Courts of Heaven: How to Present Your Case

The Jezebel Spirit: Tactics of Jezebel's Control

Heaven's Angels: The Nature and Ranking of Angels

Don't Know What to Do?: Discover Promotion in the Wilderness

Word of the Lord: Prophetic Word for 2020

The Coronavirus Prophecy

Increase Your Anointing: Discover the Supernatural

Apostolic Breakthrough: Birthing God's Purposes

The Healing Power of God: Releasing the Power of the Holy Spirit

The Secret Place of God's Power: Revelations of God's Word

The Rapture: Details of the Second Coming of Christ

Increase of Revelation and Restoration: Reveal, Recover & Restore

Restoration of the Soul: The Presence of God Changes Everything

Building a Prototype Church: The Church is in a Season of Profound of Change

Keys to Receiving Your Miracle: Miracles Happen Today

The Resurrection Power of God: Great Exploits of God

Transitioning to the Prototype Church: The Church is in a Season of Profound of Transition

Waves of Revival: Expect the Unexpected

The Stronghold of Jezebel: A True Story of a Man's Journey

Glory: Pursuing God's Presence: Revealing Secrets

Like a Mighty Rushing Wind

Steps to Revival

Supernatural Power

The Goodness of God

The Secret to Spiritual Strength

The Glorious Church's Birth: Understanding God's Plan For Our Lives

God's Presence Has a Profound Impact On Us

Spiritual Battles of the Mind: When All Hell Breaks Loose, Heaven Sends Help

A Godly Shaking Coming to the Church: Churches are Being Rerouted

Relationship with God in a New Way

The Spirit of God's Anointing: Using the Holy Spirit's Power in You

The Magnificent Church: God's Power Is Being Manifested

Miracles Are Awakened: Today is a Day of Miracles

Prepared to Fight: The Battle of Deliverance

The Journey of a Faithful: Adhering to the teachings of Jesus Christ

Ascension to the Top of Spiritual Mountains: Putting an End to Pain Cycles

After Divorce Recovery: When I Think of Grace, I Think of Mercy and Remarriage

A Greater Sense of God's Presence: Learn How to Make God's Glory Visible

Do Not Allow the Enemy to Steal: To a Crown of Righteousness, a Crown of Thorns

There Are Countless Churches: What is the Cause of Global Doom?

Creating a Model Church: The Church is Undergoing Considerable Upheaval

Developing Your Prophetic Ability: Creating a Flow of Pure Prophetic Intent

Christ's Limitless Riches Are Unsearchable: God Has Chosen Us to Be His Sons

Faith is a Link Between God's Might and Ours

Increasing the Presence of God: The Revival of the End-Times Is Approaching

Getting a Prophecy for Yourself: Unlocking Your Prophecies with Prophetic Keys

Getting Rid of the Jezebel Spirit: Before the Spirit Destroys You, Here's How to Overcome It!

Getting to Know Heaven's Court System: Secrets That Will Change Your Life

God's Resurrected Presence: Revival Glory is Being Released

God's Presence In His Kingdom: Secrets to Becoming Christ's Ambassadors

God's Healing Ability: The Holy Spirit's Power is Being Released

God's Power of Resurrection: God's Great Exploits

Heaven's Supreme Court: Providing Equal Justice for All

Increasing God's Presence in Our Lives: God's Glory Has Reached New Heights

Jezebel's Stronghold: This is the Story of an Actual Man's Journey

Making the Shift to the Model Church: The Church Is In the Midst of a Major Shift

Overcoming Lust's Influence: The Way to Victory

Pursuing God's Presence: Disclosing Information

The Plan to Take Over America: Restoring, We the People and the Power of God

Revelation and Restoration Are Increasing: The Process That Reveals, Recovers, and Restores

Burn In the Presence of the Lord

Revival Tidal Waves: Be Prepared for the Unexpected

Taking down the Demonic Realm: Curses and Revelations of Demonic Spirits

The Apocalypse: Details about Christ's Second Coming

The Hidden Resource of God's Power

The Open Doors of Satan: Access is Restricted

The Secrets to Getting Your Miracle

The Truth About Deception and Its Consequences

The Universal World: Discover the Mysteries of Heaven

Warning to the World: Details of Prophecies Have Been Revealed

Wonders and Significance: God's Glory in New Waves

Word of the Lord

Why Is There No Lasting Revival: It's Time For the Next Move of God

A Double New Beginning: A Prophetic Word, the Best Is Yet to Come

Your Most Productive Season Ever: The Anointing to Get Things Done

Break Free From Prison: No More Bondage for the Saints

Breaking Strongholds: Taking Steps to Freedom

Carrying the Glory of God: Igniting the End Time Revival

Breakthrough Over the Enemies Attack on Resources: An Angel Called Breakthrough

Days of Breakthrough: Your Time is Now

Empowered For the Unprecedented: Extraordinary Days Ahead

The Ultimate Guide to Self-Publishing: How to Write, Publish, and Promote Your Book for Free

The Art of Writing: A Comprehensive Guide to Crafting Your Masterpiece

The Non-Fiction Writer's Guide: Mastering Engaging Narratives

Spiritual Leadership (Large Print Edition): Kingdom Foundation Principles

Desperate for God's Presence (Large Print Edition): Understanding Supernatural Atmospheres

From Writer to Marketer: How to Successfully Promote Your Self-Published Book

Unleashing Your Inner Author: A Step-by-Step Guide to Crafting Your Own Bestseller

Becoming a YouTube Sensation: A Guide to Success

Watch for more at https://revivalwavesofgloryministries.com/.

About the Author

Bill Vincent is no stranger to understanding the power of God. Not only has he spent over twenty years as a Minister with a strong prophetic anointing, he is now also an Apostle and Author with Revival Waves of Glory Ministries in Litchfield, IL. Along with his wife, Tabitha, he, leads a team providing apostolic oversight in all aspects of ministry, including service, personal ministry and Godly character.

Bill offers a wide range of writings and teachings from deliverance, to experiencing presence of God and developing Apostolic cutting edge Church structure. Drawing on the power of the Holy Spirit through years of experience in Revival, Spiritual Sensitivity, and deliverance ministry, Bill now focuses mainly on pursuing the Presence of God and breaking the power of the devil off of people's lives.

His books 50 and counting has since helped many people to overcome the spirits and curses of Satan. For more information or to keep up with Bill's latest releases, please visit www.revivalwavesofgloryministries.com. To contact Bill, feel free to follow him on twitter @revivalwaves.

Read more at https://revivalwavesofgloryministries.com/.

About the Publisher

Accepting manuscripts in the most categories. We love to help people get their words available to the world.

Revival Waves of Glory focus is to provide more options to be published. We do traditional paperbacks, hardcovers, audio books and ebooks all over the world. A traditional royalty-based publisher that offers self-publishing options, Revival Waves provides a very author friendly and transparent publishing process, with President Bill Vincent involved in the full process of your book. Send us your manuscript and we will contact you as soon as possible.

Contact: Bill Vincent at rwgpublishing@yahoo.com

CPSIA information can be obtained
at www.ICGtesting.com
Printed in the USA
BVHW031049180423
662564BV00016B/1399